PRAYING
THE STATIONS
OF THE CROSS
FOR SENIORS

JOHN VAN BEMMEL

TWENTY-THIRD PUBLICATIONS A division of Bayard
One Montauk Avenue, Suite 200 · New London, CT 06320
(800) 321-0411 · www.twentythirdpublications.com

If using these stations in a group setting, the designated leader can announce the station and lead the group in the traditional opening:

We adore you O Christ and we bless you, for by your holy cross you have redeemed the world.

The leader can read the first paragraph about Jesus, and another reader can read the second paragraph. Then all can say the station's prayer together.

Opening Prayer

God, your Son never grew old. He can't teach us about getting old, can he? What can Jesus' saving death—as premature as it was—teach us about advancing years, about loneliness, about arthritis, failing eyesight, failing energy, and failing memory, about rising costs and fixed income, about the tide of uncertainties that seems to swell over us with each year?

Father, even though Jesus did not grow old, I can sense that there are tender and poignant lessons for me in his last hours. His passion and death, which I ponder in these stations of the cross, reveal, above all, that fullness of life is attained not so much by its length as by its intensity and faithfulness.

I pray these stations now, God, because I believe that Jesus will illuminate what it means to age with faith and patience, with spiritual vigor and true wisdom, with cheerfulness and generosity, with optimism and abiding hope. As Abraham and Sarah, and Zechariah and Elizabeth learned, old age is not just a time of diminishment but a time of fulfillment and challenge as well. From Jesus' passion and death, I will take comfort in this all the days of my life. Amen.

The First Station

T he finality of Pilate's words seared Jesus' soul: sentenced to die by crucifixion, a criminal's death. Only hours earlier, in the stark loneliness of Gethsemane, Jesus accepted without reservation all that his Father would ask of him: "Not my will, but yours be done." Fear-filled but composed, Jesus embraced the death sentence and so fulfilled his years in the loving surrender of his life.

As we age, we may come to see our advancing years as a fate we are sentenced to. We often rebel against the common-sense course of nature; for all creatures—stars, swans, and snakes—are born, grow old, and die. But if we can learn to embrace our aging as Jesus did his cross, our old age can be so much more than a fate to be tolerated; it can be an opportunity for continuing growth into the life and love of God.

*God, by your grace, open my eyes
to the true meaning of aging.
Let me embrace it joyously,
as my true birthright, as a challenge
to develop in wisdom and grace.
Amen.*

The Second Station

JESUS ACCEPTS HIS CROSS

The fear he felt in Gethsemane becomes cold reality as Jesus feels the heavy beam of the cross on his beaten shoulders. What was only fear now begins to be actual pain. This burden also leaves no doubt that crucifixion is unavoidable. Whatever anticipation there may have been about his fate, it will now, over the next few hours, dissolve into naked reality. Jesus will accept each phase of his execution as it comes. His heart, strained with love and pain, is open to all who will follow on this path to Calvary.

Jesus faced a moment when fear became reality, but we do not enter "old age" at a similar set point in life. The signs of slowing down, the stronger eyeglasses, the increase of aches and pains, the loss of friends and independence—these occur gradually, at different ages, with lighter or heavier burdens for different people. But however these signs come to us, and however the unavoidable reality of aging sets in, how important it is to keep our minds and hearts open to what these years will bring: the satisfaction and joys as well as the heartaches and pains. With the wisdom of our years, we move from fear to reality with an upbeat frame of mind.

*In Jesus' name, God, grace me to be realistic
about my age. Help me to grip the reality of these years,
to face my circumstances as they are, and to make
the most of them. They are, Compassionate Parent,
the path you have given me to come to you.
Amen.*

The Third Station

JESUS FALLS THE FIRST TIME

A s often as we contemplate the weakened, weary Jesus falling to the dust, we focus on the pain of collapsing under the heavy wood and suffering still more bruises. What was most difficult and painful, in fact, was not the falling but the getting up. As he was whipped into rising to reassume his cross and continue toward Calvary, Jesus had to rely on inner strength, on his character and motivation, to go on.

Not many people are inclined to view their senior years as a time of renewal and positive accomplishments. We may be tempted to see this phase of life only as going downhill both physically and psychologically. But even though we may "fall" in this sense, there are many occasions when we "get up again" and go on productively with life. We must never settle for the idea that old age is a time when nothing significant happens anymore. There is much more to each day than getting through it. This is still a time for new insights, for personal relationships, for creative activities, for deeper wisdom, and for richer spirituality.

*God, by your grace, may I rise from
the discouragement I sometimes feel.
May I go on through this time of my life
with a profound sense of renewal and grateful
anticipation for each new day you give me to love,
to create, to ponder, to converse, to learn,
and to speak with you. Amen.*

The Fourth Station

JESUS MEETS HIS MOTHER

T he sensitive, wrenching moment when Jesus' eyes met his mother's was part of his bereavement, not hers. She would soon grieve over the loss of her son, but now, the grief was his. One of Jesus' followers betrayed him, another denied he knew him, and the rest abandoned Jesus when his need was the greatest. Except for Mary and John, Jesus was alone.

It is obvious that one of the deepest sorrows of advancing years is increasing bereavement and the resulting sense of aloneness. Our parents, our spouse, our brothers and sisters, our friends, and others we know may die. Sometimes death even takes our children. Memories become more important and take up more of our day as we cling, in the only way now available, to those we knew and loved. At times, only our faith in God's presence comforts us, and our anticipation of that time when, in Thomas More's words to Margaret, his daughter, "We shall meet merrily in heaven."

God, I believe that you are with me
when I feel alone, just as you were
with Jesus in his lonely Passion.
Comfort me with the awareness
that you are faithful and that
your presence is forever. Amen.

The Fifth Station

SIMON HELPS JESUS CARRY THE CROSS

"Why me?" Jesus heard the angry protest over the noise of the crowd. In his pain, he didn't pay attention to it until a soldier brought Simon over to him. Then he understood. As Simon walked along the narrow street, he was pressed to the side to make way for the faltering Jesus and the soldiers. Just then, one of the soldiers grabbed Simon and pushed him over to help the condemned man. Simon objected: "Why should I be chosen for this? Why not somebody else? It's not fair!" Jesus understood how he felt, as Simon, for a time, took the weight of the crossbeam on his own shoulders.

The tendency to resent our misfortunes does not fade away as we age. Even with the benefit of our experience and wisdom, we still want to ask with indignation, "Why me?" when we break a hip or develop glaucoma, or find the time we hoped would be spent in leisure given over to taking care of our own elderly parents or raising our grandchildren or worrying about decisions our children have made. Jesus understands the feelings that make us want to protest, "Why me? It's not fair!" But Jesus will be with us to help us bear our crosses, just as Simon was there to help him carry his.

*Comfort me, God, when I feel unfairly put upon
or called to do things I thought I had left behind.
Help me to realize that even now I can grow through
challenge, pain, and hardship. Help me to find moments
of grace in even the most difficult situations, and fill me
with a sense of your reassuring presence. Amen.*

The Sixth Station

VERONICA WIPES THE FACE OF JESUS

Not many of Jesus' friends were around since his arrest the night before. Where were those who cheered him and laid palms in his path only days earlier? Now, on the way to his crucifixion, it was safer not to recognize Jesus or show concern for him. But courageous Veronica steps out of the crowd to wipe his face. Did it feel cool and refreshing to Jesus, or did it sting his bloodied face? Either way, Jesus saw the compassionate heart that prompted her act and was grateful for it.

As we get older, hard as it is to admit and accept, our dependence on others tends to increase. We need more and more people to offer to help us in many ways. Our children, or relatives or neighbors, increasingly become caregivers. Not all offers to help, of course, are welcome, and not all "help" is really helpful, but how loving it can be to accept an offer of help or to decline an offer graciously, to speak openly and gently about what really would ease our path. Like Jesus, we should look to the heart of the one who steps forward to help.

*God, I have spent a lifetime learning
to be a giver. Now, I need to learn the lesson of
becoming a gracious receiver. Open my heart not only to
your gifts, but to the gifts—and good intentions—
of those who care for me. Amen.*

The Seventh Station

JESUS FALLS THE SECOND TIME

Wouldn't it be understandable for Jesus to become immersed in his own suffering and fear as he falls again amid the street throng? "Who cares about these people," he might think, "about Simon and Veronica who helped me, even about my mother? All I can think about is the pain I feel and the sharp sense of being so alone." With each step and each fall, Jesus is tempted to think of himself as the only one with real pain and real problems, as the only one who matters.

How easy it is—and how human—to think only of ourselves when our problems and physical ailments burn their way into our consciousness. We become absorbed with a painful hip and a lonely week, and we miss the opportunity to console the recently widowed friend. We get so preoccupied with pouting over a grandchild's fresh remark that we forget the date we made to go shopping with a neighbor. The fact is, concern for the sorrow and pain of others may help to take us out of the narrow world of our own suffering. We lighten the burden of our years when we take on the burdens of others. Was there more on Jesus' mind than his own suffering?

God, may I never, by your grace, become so taken up
with my own problems that I become blind
and insensitive to the needs of others.
Help me in my trials to be compassionate to those
who need me, even as Jesus was,
especially in his Passion. Amen.

The Eighth Station

THE WOMEN CONSOLE JESUS

T he small group of women approached Jesus as he struggled in the procession moving slowly toward Calvary. It was their custom as "professional mourners" to try to console the condemned man and even, we are told, offer a narcotic drink to dull the pain of crucifixion. Jesus accepts their words of comfort but, we may assume, not the drug. How well that cup must have expressed the rock-bottom reality Jesus was heading for. It symbolized more clearly than the crossbeam on his back that crucifixion was indeed just ahead. That destination, that ordeal, was inevitable.

Are we not inclined to make ourselves believe that some unwelcomed events are not really going to happen? Or is it starting to dawn on us that what we thought was so far off and far-fetched in our youth is now starting to be real? All too soon, type seems to be getting much smaller, there's more gray in our hair, or much less hair, than there used to be, joints are increasingly painful.... Everyone ages and dies. What was vaguely true in our youth becomes here-and-now true for us. We have to face up to this and, like Jesus, move on in our procession toward our destination.

*God, through your grace, may I embrace with enthusiasm
the realization that I am growing old.
May the awareness of your presence be my "drug"
to spend this stage of my life in a loving,
patient, and productive way. Amen.*

The Ninth Station

JESUS FALLS THE THIRD TIME

Perhaps at the place of execution, Jesus falls yet again, exhausted physically and emotionally. Lying on the ground, Jesus finds a moment's rest before he will have to get up to face the hammer and nails. In this moment, does he recall other times he had to get up after failure and disappointment, times when he was tempted not to pursue his mission? Does he think of missed opportunities? Are there regrets about words unspoken that might have been? People who ignored his words of life? No matter now about the past. Jesus gets up again to face the present.

Let's face it—by the time we're seniors, we've known a lifetime of falls. Not just in the sense of "sins," but those regrets one amasses over the years: the career not chosen, the sweetheart not married, the impetuous business decision, the broken friendship, the hurtful words, the things that might have been. But what of those decades of wrongs and blunders? What benefit is there in mulling over them now? Self-forgiveness is the order of the day—every day of our later years. We have to pick ourselves up from our past and move boldly into the present. We can acknowledge the "might have beens," but we can't let them consume us.

God, I know you have forgiven my sins.
By your grace, help me to forgive myself and to put
behind me for good all those regrets I have carried
with me all these years. May I rise from my past and,
like Jesus, be busy with what remains to be done:
doing your will all the days of my life. Amen.

The Tenth Station

JESUS IS STRIPPED

Jesus is now stripped of his last possession. On a small hill just outside the city gates, Jesus stands naked to the world as the soldiers remove his clothes to prepare him for crucifixion. He has lost his strength, his freedom, his disciples, and now even his clothes. What more can he lose? But without owning so much as a garment to cover himself, he has not lost his self-possession and dignity. Amid the degradation and torment he suffers, we see so clearly that his fundamental value and dignity come from who he is, not from what he possesses.

Like Jesus stripped on Calvary, age makes us more and more vulnerable to so many losses. When incomes are fixed, but expenses are not, we may experience a wrenching worry about money as our sense of security is stripped away. We may find ourselves or our spouse growing vague and forgetful, and we may have to face the slow loss of the accumulated memories and shared experiences. But, no matter what losses come with old age, we know that God knows us and holds us, and in God we have everything that really matters.

*By your grace, God, I want to grow closer
to you each day. Like Jesus, I stand naked before you,
with all my worries and fears, and you see the core
of my being. Even if I should lose myself,
keep me in your care and remind me that I am
your child, loved and cherished always. Amen.*

The Eleventh Station

JESUS IS NAILED TO THE CROSS

T he grotesque act of nailing a human being to a post takes place about midday, and Jesus, one of three criminals, is raised on high. Beyond the torment, the thirst, the blood loss, and the suffocation, Jesus also hears the jeers of those who arranged his execution: "He relied on God. Now let God come to rescue him."

After a lifetime of faith in God's loving presence, we still harbor a feeling that God will rescue us from the losses and pains that old age inevitably brings. We call on God, at least implicitly, to spare us from the loss of friends, the diminishment of our health, the lack of companionship, the neglect by our family. It is just as hard now as it was years ago to understand that, yes, God will rescue us ultimately, but that God will save us not *from* these losses but *through* them. God will be with us as we grow older but not spare us from the natural effects of aging. When faced with the reality that there is no way out, we have to align ourselves with Jesus and trust that God will be with us as we hang on our crosses, and God will embrace us afterward.

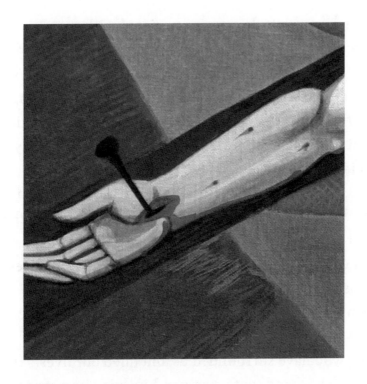

*I trust in you, God, to be with me in these
declining years as you were with Jesus on his cross.
By your grace, help me to live my remaining years
as if everything depends on me, but to believe
and to pray as if everything depends on you. Amen.*

The Twelfth Station

JESUS DIES ON THE CROSS

From multiple causes associated with the crucifixion, Jesus' life is "interrupted." What did Mary and the others think as they watched Jesus surrender to the inevitable? It was the end of a loving, faithful, composed, principled, and self-sacrificing life. What if Jesus had not died at this time, but, let us say, had taught and healed and loved for another fifteen years, and then was crucified? Would Mary's life and their lives and ours have been that much more enriched? What if...? But let us be content with God's ways.

The death of those we know always affects our lives. We become a bit poorer or even greatly diminished when associates, friends, or spouse or family members die. As our years increase, we lose more and more of those who have surrounded us and filled our lives. "If only my husband (wife, partner, brother, sister, friend) had not died...." We resent their deaths and perhaps blame them for our impoverishment. Our world has grown smaller and lonelier, and we are left with the faith that accepts the crooked lines of God's writing.

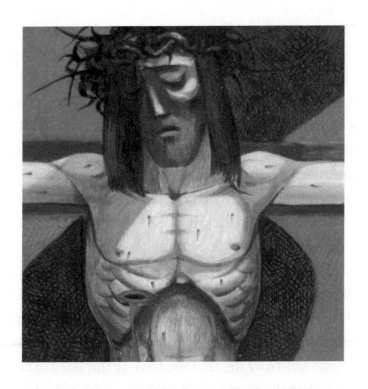

*God, I thank you for those you have given me
to enrich my life. Help me, by your grace,
to accept their passing. Though I am poorer
because of it, I rejoice that they are with you
and that I can smile at my memories of them.
Amen.*

The Thirteenth Station

JESUS IS TAKEN DOWN FROM THE CROSS

"It is finished," Jesus had said a short time earlier on the cross. Now he lay dead in Mary's arms. This emotional tableau was the model immortalized in marble by Michelangelo's *Pietà*. Jesus' life was over. Through three years, he was the model of God for many of his contemporaries, and then, over the centuries since then, for endless millions. "He who sees me, sees the Father," Jesus had said. As the model of a human life, Jesus would touch us all and leave his blessed influence on the world forever.

Our imbedded desire to be useful does not leave us in our older years. Indeed, as time grows rapidly shorter, we keenly want to be helpful. But in our heart of hearts we also want to assure ourselves that our lives have been useful and worthwhile, that we have influenced others for good, that the world is a better place for the love we have left in it, and that we have, to some degree at least, been a model of human living. And until it is time to say, "It is finished," we can continue to live a life of love.

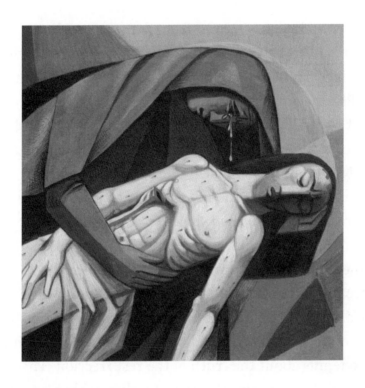

*God, I thank you for allowing me to be your instrument
to accomplish the good I have done and am still doing.
May I, through your grace, continue to use
my mind and body, my talents, and my aspirations
for your purposes. Amen.*

The Fourteenth Station

JESUS IS LAID IN THE TOMB

Jesus' body was removed from the execution site and brought to a tomb cut out of rock. One of those who helped prepare the body for burial was Nicodemus, the Pharisee who had questioned Jesus secretly one night a couple of years earlier about his teaching and miracles. Jesus spoke of himself as being "lifted up." Did Nicodemus connect this with being lifted up on the cross? Gazing at the lifeless body of Jesus, did he also recall that Jesus had spoken of rising three days later? Did Nicodemus believe this would happen?

Increasingly, as we get older and feel more and more the effects of aging—we begin to acknowledge our mortality. We may not dwell on it, but it begins to take up residence at our side. Perhaps we wonder with Nicodemus about the truth of the resurrection. This is where faith comes in. Our faith teaches us that the cross was not the end. As we have all been "lifted up" on our daily cross, we also trust that we will rise to new life with Jesus. This faith in our ultimate victory overshadows the other joys and sorrows of our remaining years.

*God, swell my being
with faith in your desire
to bring me to yourself.
By your grace, help me
in these diminishing years
to be a person of faith:
faith in your continuing
presence now, and faith
that your eternal presence
comes from my dying
and rising with your Son,
my Lord Jesus. Amen.*

CLOSING PRAYER

God, as I step slowly along my way of the cross
through the years you give me, grace me to
appreciate each day's opportunities to love and
to be productive, to feel your presence when I am
burdened with the sorrows that accompany aging.
Grace me to open my heart to your still-strange
ways and to rise above my recent and long-ago
failures. Grace me with the realization that you
value me for who I am, and that I am always
precious in your sight. Grace me, God, with the
awareness that the richness of my remaining
years is measured by my faithfulness in you.

God, through Jesus' passion and death, may
I come to recognize that these years of both
growth and diminishment will lead finally to
you. By your grace, I trust that my way of the
cross will bring me, as Jesus' did, to resurrection
and to fullness of life with you forever.

Amen.